# BLUE SKIES AND BUTTERFLIES:

## HOW MONARCHS EAT A LOT, SLEEP, AND WAKE UP BEAUTIFUL

### AND MANY MORE FASCINATING FACTS

by Holly Trueman Urie

3BEES PRESS

A

Publication

Published by 3Bees Press, Boca Raton, FL, 2019

First Printing August 2019

ISBN-13:  978-1089542704
ISBN-10:  1089542704

# CONTENTS

# INTRODUCTION

**W**elcome to the amazing and incomparable world of the North American monarch butterfly! If butterflies are new to you, then this may be the beginning of a lifelong adventure that only gets better as you dig deeper and learn more. A trip to the park or a walk in your own backyard garden will take on new dimensions as you begin to notice each and every butterfly that finds its way into your path. And even if the world of butterfly watching is not new to you, the miraculous process of metamorphosis — egg to caterpillar to chrysalis to butterfly — never fails to fascinate or pique the curiosity of novices and butterfly aficionados alike.

Scientists are discovering new and different species all the time but estimate that there are somewhere in the neighborhood of 17,000 different species of butterflies in the world, all of which belong to the scientific order of Lepidoptera. Of these, approximately 750 different species have been found in North America north of Mexico. About 575 of those have been seen in the lower 48 states of the United States, and 275 have been found in Canada.

Of the three known species of monarch butterflies, *Danaus plexippus*, as described in 1758 by the Swedish botanist, physician, and zoologist Carl Linnaeus, is the species now known most commonly as the North American monarch. Whether part of the eastern North American population, the western North American population, or even the non-migratory populations found in Georgia and Florida, the monarch is the most beloved and recognizable butterfly in North America. Originally native to both North and South America, this species began to spread abroad in the 1840's and can now be found in Spain, Portugal, Australia, New Zealand, part of the South Pacific, and Hawaii. Most recently, monarchs even accompanied scientists on flights to the International Space Station!

As its name suggests, the monarch is recognized by many to be the "king of all butterflies." It is graceful and regal in flight, with distinctive orange, black, and white markings to set it apart. Beautiful, harmless, and even symbolic, monarchs are unique and rise above all the others in a number of significant ways. For example, unlike the

MONARCH n. 1: one who reigns over a kingdom or an empire; 2: one holding preeminent position or power. *(Merriam-Webster Dictionary)*

garden-destroying caterpillars of many butterfly species, monarch caterpillars prefer milkweed and milkweed only. Consequently, they will never be found destroying summer vegetable gardens. Symbolic of rebirth, joy, the miracle of life, and transformation, monarchs are the butterfly of choice for wedding ceremonies. Even their uniquely beautiful chrysalis — brilliant jade green and trimmed out in a fine, golden thread — is incomparable. However, perhaps most amazing of all, the monarch's life cycle stands alone in the world of butterflies, where researchers have yet to pinpoint and explain the science behind their extraordinary life cycle and migratory behaviors.

American fascination with this amazing flying insect is on the upswing as awareness of its plight increases — i.e., a 90-percent drop in population since 1990. *Save the Monarch* campaigns are in place across the country to educate the public as the US Fish and Wildlife Service continues its evaluation to determine whether the North American monarch qualifies for classification as an endangered species according to the guidelines set forth in the Endangered Species Act. There are numerous ways for individuals and groups alike to contribute to the gigantic effort underway to help this beautiful North American icon before it is too late. Hopefully, this book will be a jumping-off point for you, too, and that armed with additional knowledge, you will be able to make your own contributions to saving the monarch.

Image: USDA/NRCS

# IN THE BEGINNING ...

**M**ore often than not, a memorable first experience with raising monarchs ignites the desire to do so over and over again. Perhaps a friend or acquaintance has given you a milkweed plant loaded with several tiny black-, white-, and yellow-striped monarch caterpillars, or maybe you just found several larger ones on the underside of milkweed leaves in your own yard and you are helping an excited child pack them up to bring into school. Whatever the source of your first catylyst may be, it is likely that you have stumbled into the process accidentally or done so voluntarily and are not sure exactly how to proceed. What you do know is that you need help right now, today, learning at least the bare minimum necessary to nurture and keep these caterpillar babies safe until their transformation is complete. Regardless of the manner, for most people who are new to monarchs and butterflies in general, the usual reaction at this point is, "What do I do now?"

This chapter will address exactly that, basic monarch survival, without jumping into extensive detail right away. More specific information will follow in subsequent chapters after the current crisis is put to rest. The study of monarchs can be very complicated and even overwhelming at times. There is so much already written about them, yet still so much more to know! Rarely, however, is there a lack of excitement and fascination following a first opportunity to personally witness a caterpillar changing into a butterfly.

The goal of this book, therefore, is to provide immediate help to the person just starting out by briefly and logically stepping through what can be expected for the next couple of weeks as these tiny caterpillars mature and progress through the fascinating process of metamorphosis. This does not mean that what follows is intended only for beginners. On the contrary, there is valuable information for all. This is simply an explanation of what may appear to be an unusual way to begin. Let's get started!

The female monarch, like all butterflies, is very selective about where she lays her eggs, and for very good reason.

**HOST PLANT:** A plant that provides the necessary nouristment needed for survival by the offspring of a butterfly species. Milkweed is the only plant on which a female monarch will lay her eggs because she knows it is the only food source on which her hatchlings will be able to survive.

*Giant Milkweed*
*Asclepias gigantea*

The baby caterpillars that will emerge in three or four days from the tiny eggs she has deposited can only survive on the singular host plant that is appropriate for her species, which in the case of the monarch is milkweed.

All butterflies require two types of plants over the course of their lifespan, and the monarch is no different. Nectar plants are the food source for adult butterflies, while host plants are the only plants able to support the hungry baby caterpillars that will emerge from eggs deposited by the female butterfly. Nectar plants are flowering plants from which the adult butterfly will use its proboscis — a coiled straw-like tongue — to literally sip the nectar out of the flowers.

Unfortunately, nectar plants other than milkweed itself are not of any help when the female is in search of an ideal plant on which to lay her eggs. When she is ready, the adult female monarch will seek out only one kind of plant, milkweed. She will do this because she knows that the baby caterpillars that hatch out of the eggs she will deposit on the underside of the milkweed leaves cannot survive without milkweed leaves to eat. Amazingly, Mother Nature even provides a way for her to find the right kind of plant. By drumming her legs against the surface of a leaf, the female monarch is able to cause the plant to release genetic chemicals that are picked up by her own chemoreceptors. Stimulation of these chemoreceptors will set in motion the desired response at this point. She will begin to lay her eggs. If, however, she has landed on a snapdragon, for example, her chemoreceptors will let her know that she must move on, and she will keep doing so until she again detects the chemical unique to milkweed. Once deposited, the eggs will begin to hatch in approximately three or four days.

Monarchs are voracious eaters! During the next 10 to 14 days, your caterpillars will grow from the size of a pinhead to almost 2 inches in length. That is an astounding 2,000-percent growth rate in less than 2 weeks, during which time they will repeatedly devour and strip their milkweed plants down to the stalks. As the growing caterpillar approaches the end of this larval stage and

**NECTAR PLANTS:**
Flowering plants whose nectar is the food source for adult butterflies.

nears the chrysalis stage, it is not uncommon to find a fresh, new plant completely stripped to nothing in a matter of a few overnight hours. It is therefore important to have extra plants or leaves ready to swap out so that everyone is kept well fed and growing.

The easiest way to replace a chewed-up plant without handling or hurting any growing caterpillars that still may be attached to the stalks is to clip off that part of the stalk of the chewed-up plant that still contains caterpillars and place it near the stalk of the new plant. Hungry cats will find their way to the fresh leaves in no time. For real emergencies, spare milkweed leaves will also remain surprisingly fresh if kept refrigerated in an airtight plastic bag. This can be a real lifesaver if no complete plants are readily available when needed.

During this period of extreme growth, you will notice that your caterpillars seem to be shedding their skins every now and then. This process is called molting, and it will actually happen five times between hatchling and chrysalis. Each of these growth periods is called an instar (development period), during which time you might also notice your caterpillars suspending their eating as they search for an ideal place to molt. Once the molt is complete, it is not uncommon to catch them eating the nutrition-filled skins they have just shed before they head back to the milkweed plant to begin the next instar. The fifth and final instar stage, however, is a little different and will result in the formation of an emerald-green chrysalis.

By the time a caterpillar reaches Instar 3, it will be approximately one-half inch in length. It is during the final stages, Instar 4 and Instar 5, that the most dramatic growth will be realized. As it approaches the end of development during this larval stage (approximately two inches in length and quite chubby), your caterpillar will stop eating, leave the plant, and begin looking for a good place on which to affix itself in preparation for Instar 5 chrysalis formation. When cages are used, you will see them climbing up the sides to reach the top, much flatter surface. In nature, they will instinctively seek an overhang or horizontal branch that is sturdy enough to meet their needs.

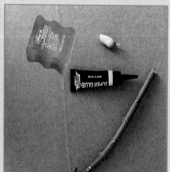

2000% Growth in Two Weeks

At this point, the caterpillar will attach itself to the surface and hang upside-down in a "J" shape for 12 to 14 hours, culminating in its fifth and final molt, Instar 5, which will leave it enveloped in a glossy, jade-colored chrysalis that is trimmed in a fine, golden thread.

Over the course of another 10 to 14 days, an amazing change will take place inside this chrysalis as the caterpillar transforms into its butterfly form. As the monarch's time to eclose (emerge) draws near, the chrysalis will first begin to darken and then become more and more transparent as faint hints of orange and black become visible. This can happen rather quickly as the end approaches. First, a crack will appear in the shell, but within a minute or two the monarch will burst out of its chrysalis skin, crumpled and damp.

As it hangs upside from what remains of its chrysalis, the new monarch will begin to pump its wings in order to fill them with liquids stored in its body for that purpose. Within 30 minutes, the wings will be fully expanded, but it will take another hour or two before the butterfly is ready for flight. Fluttering wings will signal that it is time to go!

Hopefully, this brief outline has gotten you successfully through your first experience with the amazing life cycle of the monarch butterfly. In fact, at this point and after perhaps experiencing a first taste of "butterfly frenzy," most people become hooked and want to know more about this sometimes complicated, but always amazing, display of one of nature's beauties. The chapters that follow will delve into more specific details as well as answer some of the many questions that inevitably arise at this point.

## Sometimes Things Go Wrong ...

### Chrysalis falls to the ground or the bottom of the cage

It is essential for the newly emerged butterfly to be able to hang upside down to stretch its wings and dry out when it emerges. A fallen chrysalis can be easily re-hung to reposition it to accommodate this. SuperGlue and/or dental floss make the repair very easy. If there is enough silk left on the cremaster (top of the chrysalis), loop a piece of dental floss around the silk and tighten. Tie to a secure place, allowing sufficient stretching room for the adult that will soon emerge. If the break at the top has left nothing large enough to tie to, use a small drop of SuperGlue to first affix the dental floss. When dry, floss is ready to re-hang the chrysalis.

### Chrysalis darkens but butterfly does not emerge after 48 hours

Once darkened, the butterfly is usually ready and should eclose within a day or so. If a darkened chrysalis still remains intact after 48 hours, it is safe to assume that the monarch is either dead or very sick and will not make it. Place it in a plastic bag in the freezer for 48 hours to euthanize if there is any uncertainty.

# MONARCH ANATOMY

**B**utterflies, including monarch butterflies, are among the group of insects that undergoes complete metamorphosis. Insects that experience complete metamorphosis typically look markedly different during their immature phases than they do when they reach adulthood. Several stages of development are involved (from least mature to adult): egg, multiple larval instars, pupa, and winged adult.

## EGG

**M**onarch eggs are laid individually by the female usually on the underside of a milkweed leaf, although from time to time a stray egg may be found on top of a leaf or flower. The outer shell is hard so as to protect the developing larva, and the inside is lined with wax to prevent drying out. Eggs are the size of a pinhead and will be very pale green or light cream in color. Each egg weighs less than 0.5 mg and is conical shaped with raised ridges running vertically, top to bottom. Eggs will hatch within a week. A black nub developing at the tip of the egg is a good indicator that the caterpillar is about to emerge.

## LARVA
### Caterpillar

**T**he caterpillar is the butterfly's larval stage. Like the adult butterfly that it will eventually become, the larva has the same distinct body parts, albeit different in form and structure:

### HEAD

The head includes a pair of very short antennae; mouth parts, including the upper and lower lips and the mandibles; and six pairs of eyes. The eyes, also called ocelli, are very simple so the caterpillar's vision is very poor. Antennae are present to help guide the poor-visioned caterpillar, while sensory organs called the maxillary palps help direct food into its mouth. Chubby filaments at the front and back of the caterpillar are also sensory organs, but they are separate from the antennae and should not be confused.

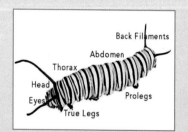

METAMORPHOSIS:
Developmental process
for insects that changes
as each new level of
maturity is reached: Egg
to larva (caterpillar) to pupa
(chrysalis) to adult butterfly.

## THORAX

The thorax is the middle section between the head at the front and the abdomen at the back. Each of the three thoracic segments has a pair of jointed legs. These are considered true legs and should be differentiated from the prolegs that are found on the abdomen. Holes located in the sides of both the thorax and the abdomen are called spiracles and connect to a system of airtubes that provides oxygen for breathing.

## ABDOMEN

The abdomen is the last section. All abdominal segments do not have legs, but the 5 segments that do have legs have prolegs, which are actually false legs. Prolegs have tiny hooks that allow the larva to grip and hold tight to a leaf or its silk mat. Spiracles are also present for breathing.

When the caterpillar is between 10 and 14 days old, it will be ready to enter its next amazing phase. It will stop eating and usually leave the milkweed plant completely as it seeks an appropriate place to pupate.

# PUPA
## Chrysalis

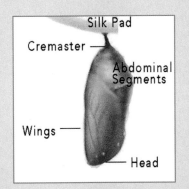

A full-grown caterpillar will naturally seek out a flat, safe surface on which to attach itself, which more often than not will be the top of its cage or screened enclosure when raised in captivity. Even the manner in which the monarch caterpillar attaches itself is nothing short of an amazing achievement. Once satisfied that it has found the best place possible, the caterpillar will spin on that spot a tiny button of silk-like material. It will then turn itself completely around so that it can attach its tail-end to this silky nub. Now securely attached, it will hang upside-down in a shape that resembles a "J" for another 10 to 15 hours.

As the end of this "J" period approaches, the caterpillar will begin to twitch a bit and straighten ever so slightly, which is often a clue that one of the most fascinating parts of its transformation is about to occur. Its skin will appear to open up in a zipper-like fashion revealing a pale-green pupa as the fifth and final molt (Instar 5) begins. In what some call the "pupa dance," over the next minute or two the hanging caterpillar will whirl and twirl until what was once a chubby little caterpillar becomes a beautiful jade-green chrysalis that is trimmed in gold.

## ADULT
### Butterfly

All butterflies, including the monarch, have three body parts, six jointed legs, one pair of antennae, compound eyes, and an exoskeleton. As members of the order of Lepidoptera, they are flying insects with large, scaly wings. The three body parts are:

## HEAD

The head consists of a pair of antennae, a proboscis, and two compound eyes.

• *Antennae*: The antennae serve a number of purposes. First, they play a critical role in both the search for food and the search for a mate. They also act as a clock that signals the onset of nightfall and a reminder that it is time to rest. Lastly, but certainly not of lesser importance, the base of the antennae is connected to the Johnston's organ. Unique to all butterflies, this organ controls balance and is responsible for the butterfly's ability to right itself on a windy day.

• *Proboscis*: This coiled mouth part is very flexible, and its strawlike structure uncoils to allow the butterfly to drink water and suck nectar from flowering plants.

• *Eyes*: Butterflies have two sets of eyes. One pair of simple, single-chambered eyes is used primarily for determining brightness, while a second set, their compound eyes, are comprised of thousands of light receptors and microscopic lenses that work together to create a mosaic view of what the butterfly finds in its line of sight.

Proboscis out and ready to nectar

## THORAX

This center portion of the adult butterfly's three-part body structure is further divided into three more sections.

• *Legs*: To each of the three sections is attached a pair of jointed legs. The foot of each leg is clawlike to facilitate grasping. Legs have sense organs that are used to taste food as the butterfly flits from plant to plant as well as chemoreceptors to help the female butterfly determine whether she has found an appropriate place to lay her eggs. The front pair of legs often has the added job of keeping the antennae clean. Leg movement is controlled by muscles in the thorax.

• *Wings*: Also attached to the thorax are the wings. All butterflies have four wings — two attached to the middle section of the thorax (forewings) and two attached to the last section (hindwings). The wings are made of very thin layers of chitlin, a protein similar to the material in human hair and nails. Butterfly wings are connected and strengthened by a system of tiny fibers and blood vessels that enable them to work together in unison during flight.

• *Scales*: The wing membrane is further protected by a layer of thousands of tiny scales. Rapid contraction and expansion of muscles at the point of connection to the thorax cause the wings to move during flight. These tiny scales are also responsible for the various colors and markings that differentiate the thousands of varieties of butterflies. Finally, the scales provide insulation, which in turn helps the butterfly soak up the heat of the sun for warmth, especially during migration.

## ABDOMEN

The soft abdomen is divided into 11 segments, some readily visible but a few fused and more difficult to differentiate. It contains a simple, flexible, tube-like heart; Malpighian tubules used for excretion; reproductive organs (claspers or ovipositors); breathing spores called spiracles; and most of the digestive system.

# METAMORPHOSIS

As they grow, many insects, including butterflies, change in form through a process called *metamorphosis*. The life cycle of each individual monarch is therefore divided into four distinct stages of growth; but as a species, monarchs will also go through four generations every year. (This does get a little confusing, but keep reading because it will become clearer!)

The four stages that make up the life cycle of each individual monarch butterfly are the egg, the larva (caterpillar), the pupa (chrysalis), and the adult butterfly. The four generations that the species cycles through each year are actually represented by at least four different butterflies working their way through each of these four life-cycle stages — egg, larva, pupa, and adult — during one complete year. Once this cycle is complete, it will repeat itself year after year with the first generation ready to begin the four stages of the life cycle all over again.

### METAMORPHOSIS
Egg to Caterpillar (Larva) to Chrysalis (Pupa) to Adult Butterfly

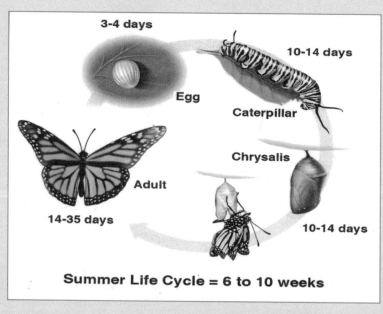

*Image: US Fish and Wildlife Service*

# REPRODUCTION AND LIFE CYCLE

## REPRODUCTION

As with most living organisms, butterfly reproduction is the result of the female's eggs being fertilized by sperm provided by a male butterfly. The male will connect to the female via a clasping organ called the clasper located on his abdomen. Once connected, this process can take up to 16 hours as the male monarch deposits sperm into a sac called the bursa located on the female's abdomen. Sperm is stored in this sac until it is time for her to lay her eggs, at which time the most recently deposited sperm will be used to individually fertilize each egg as it is deposited on the host plant.

In all butterfly species, fertilized eggs are deposited on or near the appropriate host plants in a variety of different ways depending on the species. Some eggs are deposited in small clusters, while others are left in large batches of up to 100 eggs. Some are laid singly, one at a time. Each female may lay hundreds of eggs before her job is finished, with the bulk of her work usually being carried out during her first three or four days of life.

Once again, the monarch's behavior is just a little bit different as the monarch female prefers a more personal touch, individually depositing each egg one at a time, usually, although not always, on the underside of a very carefully selected milkweed leaf. Eggs may also occasionally be found on the top of a leaf or even on milkweed flowers. Eggs are ribbed, yellowish-white, and oval shaped, and each egg is about the size of the head of a pin.

If you have ever wondered why the female seems so busy, it is probably because she is! Female monarchs begin mating when they are 3 or 4 days old and will start laying eggs within a few days. A typical female can deposit as many as 200 eggs in a single day and up to 500 by the time she has finished her task after several days of work. Large quantities are necessary for the survival of the species as only about 20 percent of these eggs — that is, about 2 out of every 10 — reach maturity and go on to become adult butterflies.

Predators abound in the form of ants, wasps and other insects, birds, and even other monarch caterpillars, all attacking the eggs and newly hatched babies. It is not at all uncommon to find mature caterpillars happily munching on milkweed leaves that have been very recently visited by an egg-laying female monarch. These eggs may never get the opportunity to hatch if they happen to be on the underside of a leaf that is in the path of a growing caterpillar busily stripping the plant of all of its leaves.

Monarchs also experience reproductive diapause, which is a temporary stage of development where they postpone sexual activities in order to store up energy for their anticipated migration. For this reason, good nectar sources become more important than even milkweed during the early fall as the monarchs begin to anticipate their forthcoming migratory journey and the extra energy they will need.

# LIFE CYCLE

**M**onarch reproduction and life cycle are very closely linked. For this reason, it is especially important to understand their *reproductive process as a species over the course of an entire year*. A clear understanding of this life cycle is critical to understanding how monarchs differ from other butterflies. While some of the following summary at first glance may appear to be a little repetitive, its importance merits repetition and overlap discussions in order to paint the clearest picture possible.

Once the female has deposited her eggs, each individual monarch will go through the following stages:

- Female monarch deposits eggs on milkweed plants.

- Eggs hatch 3 or 4 days later.

- Near-microscopic newly hatched caterpillar feeds on milkweed for the next 10 to 14 days, eventually growing to approximately 2 inches and devouring enough milkweed each day to equal its own body weight.

- Caterpillar sheds its skin 5 times during this period in order to accommodate rapid growth.

- Full-grown caterpillar leaves the milkweed plant and seeks a place to pupate. After attaching itself to a smooth surface, it hangs in a "J" shape for approximately 14 hours.

- Caterpillar sheds its skin (molt) for a final time and passes to the pupa (chrysalis) stage, where it is encased in a protective jade-green shell about an inch in length and from which the fully formed butterfly will eventually emerge.

- For the next 10 to 14 days, dramatic changes occur within the chrysalis, transforming it from a crawling insect to one of the most beautiful of flying insects. During this time the chrysalis darkens to black and begins to thin out so that the orange insides are visible.

- The butterfly, still wet and crumpled, bursts out of its shell. It will hang upside-down for about an hour as it stretches and pumps the fluid out of its wings readying for flight.

This pattern will repeat itself four times each year — egg to caterpillar to chrysalis to butterfly — where each cycle equals one complete generation of the four that will occur that year. However, each generation is not equal, and this is yet another way that monarchs differ so distinctly from other butterflies.

# GENERATION SUMMARY
# FOR THE
# EASTERN MONARCH POPULATION

## Generation 1:

March-April

The first generation is the immediate offspring of the overwintering generation as it leaves Mexico. Eggs are laid by overwintering females from late March through most of April in northern Mexico as well as into the southern US. These females are the **same females** that made the journey south 6 to 8 months earlier during the fall migration. This generation will lay eggs through the end of May as they begin to work their way north. Metamorphosis cycle for this generation may take a week or two longer as cooler weather may still persist and slow the cycle somewhat. Adults emerge from late April through June, and some of the new adults will begin to show up in the northern states and southern Canada. Average lifespan is 2 to 4 weeks per butterfly.

## Generation 2:

May-June

Eggs from this generation are widely distributed throughout much of eastern North America from late April through June with some eggs beginning to emerge in parts of the South in early May. As they progress northward, the majority of adults emerge in June and July. Later members of this generation will continue moving north, whereas the earlier ones most likely stay put and produce as many offspring as possible. Average lifespan is 2 to 4 weeks per butterfly.

## Generation 3:

July-August

Eggs from this generation are laid throughout the entire northern range from late May through all of July. Most of those that emerge early in this cycle are able to reproduce another summer generation, but some of those born in late July may experience diapause and become part of the next southern migration. Average lifespan of those in this group will be split between the early ones at 2 to 4 weeks and those that come later and live for 6 to 8 months as part of the overwintering population.

## Generation 4:

September-October

Eggs are laid throughout all of July and August. Adults that emerge from this population will experience diapause and begin to prepare for migration by drinking extra nectar and beginning to cluster with others. Southward movement will begin in September and continue through early October as they journey toward Mexico. This generation will remain in Mexico for 6 to 8 months. They will come out of diapause in March, mate, begin their journey northward as they begin to lay eggs that become the new Generation 1 for the next year, thus starting the entire cycle all over again.

# MIGRATION

**M**igration works together with reproduction and life cycle to differentiate the monarch from every other species of butterflies, the result of which is probably the most amazing of all of the monarch's unique characteristics. Of the world's thousands of known species of butterflies, monarchs are the only species known to make an annual two-way migration. This annual migratory behavior is similar to that of many birds that head south during winter months and then return the following spring, but researchers have yet to be able to pinpoint or explain the science behind this extraordinary monarch phenomenon — both how it happens as well as why it does not appear to happen with any of the other 15,000 to 20,000 different species of butterflies on earth.

As mentioned earlier, by the time they reach adulthood, every monarch has experienced the four-stage process of metamorphosis — egg to larva to pupa to adult. Also explained was the fact that as a species, monarchs go through four of these life cycles — four generations — every year. Now to confuse this issue even further, all generations are not equal. Those that are born during the summer months typically live for 2 to 4 weeks, while the last generation of the year, the fall generation, is different and will live for 6 to 8 months under completely different living conditions than those of the earlier generations.

## How and why does this happen?

While overwintering without changing location is generally not a problem for other types of butterflies, monarchs simply cannot survive the cold northern winters. Consequently, as a species and in large numbers they travel south to seek warmer weather. Those that make this trip have never been south before. They only know that it is necessary to make the trip and how to get there because Mother Nature has built the needed know-how into them simply because they are members of this fall generation.

## How do monarch generations differ?

Butterflies that comprise the spring and summer generations live for only a few weeks each. They tend to be rather solitary in nature and are seldom seen in the company of others unless mating. Their reproductive system is fully functional, rendering them ready to mate within days of emerging from their chrysalides.

From the moment they hatch from the egg, members of the fall generation are different. Their reproductive system is somehow less developed and immature upon emergence, and they go into diapause instead of mating. They sense the need to begin preparing for their forthcoming journey and will seek out larger quantities of nectar, become more social, and begin gathering in large groups. Finally, they are much larger, weighing more and having a wingspan in excess of 4 inches compared to the average 3½ to 4 inches typical of the earlier generations.

## How do they know when to go?

Using environmental clues like shorter days, fluctuating temperatures, and less appealing milkweed, members of the fall generation intuitively know they need to prepare. In late August and early September, they begin to sense the changing length of the days; and together with the fluctuations in temperature, this somehow triggers them into diapause. These factors, along with a significant reduction in the availability and quality of milkweed necessary for their offspring to survive, cue them to delay reproduction until springtime and to instead begin their migration.

## How long does it take, and where do they go?

Between late August and October each year, masses of North American monarchs from as far away as Southern Canada begin their trek south to overwintering locations in Mexico and Southern California. Traveling only during daylight hours, masses of monarchs, sometimes numbering in the thousands, will darken late-summer and early-fall skies. Moving at speeds of between 15 and 25 mph, they will often take advantage of upper air masses called thermals to help make the trip a little bit easier. Some will travel as many as 3,000 miles, huddling close together for warmth as they stop to roost and rest overnight and then bask in the warmth of the sun before they continue their long journey the next day. The larger and stronger ones will usually make better time and arrive before those that are weaker, oftentimes landing in the exact same trees that had been occupied by the previous year's migrating generation even though they have never been there before.

There are two populations of monarchs in North America. The eastern population originates in Southern Canada and the United States east of the Rocky Mountains and travels south along several flyways that all merge into one flyway in Central Texas. From Central Texas, this single flyway will then be the one path that all will follow the remainder of the way to their overwintering sites in Central Mexico sometime in November. They will roost there until March. The western population from areas west of the Rockies will overwinter at sites along the Pacific Coast of California. It is believed that there is probably some crossing over between the two populations because tagged monarchs will occasionally be found at unexpected locations. In

Mexico, the monarchs will roost in the same 11 or 12 locations within a 73-mile region. Their roosts are located in oyamel forests high in the Sierra Madre Mountains where warm temperatures and humidity provide an ideal habitat during the winter months. To the west, the western monarch population will overwinter in 200 to 300 smaller winter colonies along the Pacific coast near Santa Cruz, San Diego, Baja, and the Sierra Nevada foothills that provide similarly comfortable habitats in eucalyptus, Monterey pine, and Monterey cypress trees. Monarchs in both Mexico and California will roost close together in large clusters to stay warm, sometimes tens of thousands on a single tree!

St. Mark's National Wildlife Refuge, Tallahassee, FL: Roosting monarchs getting ready to complete their journey to Mexico.

*Image:US Fish and Wildlife Service*

## When do they return north?

Eastern migration starts in March as warm temperatures return and days get longer. The northward journey will start as the butterflies begin to travel north, returning by way of Texas and other southern states as they progress. Diapause will end, and previously undeveloped reproductive systems will become functional. Females will begin to lay eggs along the way to start the first generation of the new year. However, unlike the single generation that made the entire trip south during the fall without reproducing, different successive generations will make the trip north. In fact, two or three more generations will be produced as the monarchs work their way to their northern homes. The southward migration will start all over again in late summer.

*Image:US Fish and Wildlife Service*

Spring migration is less dramatic in California, where the western monarchs will move inland and breed in scattered habitats throughout the West, but primarily California or wherever they can find milkweed. They will produce several generations before returning to their overwintering sites in November.

## What about Florida?

Monarchs continue to present some unanswered questions for researchers, especially in warmer climates like Florida and even the east coast of Texas. There seems to be agreement that not all monarchs

*Image:US Fish and Wildlife Service*

migrate and that migrating populations probably coexist with non-migrating populations in some areas. This is likely the case in Florida, where the monarch population seems to be comprised of at least three groups: (1) year-round, non-migratory residents; (2) residents that accidentally ended up in the state because they were sidetracked from the eastern migration passing through on its way to Mexico; and (3) some, especially in the northern part of the state, that are truly a part of the Mexico-bound migrating monarchs. And even these examples are not clear cut. For example, each year St. Mark's National Wildlife Refuge just south of Tallahassee celebrates its Monarch Butterfly Festival in late October so that visitors can witness thousands of roosting monarchs gathering before they complete the final leg of their journey to Mexico. However, even here there is debate as to how many of these butterflies actually continue on or if some remain and overwinter in Florida.

Studies being conducted in university research labs around the country (most notably the University of Minnesota, University of Kansas, University of Florida, and University of Georgia) are coming up with unexpected results in some cases. By analyzing the chemical composition of the wings of adult butterflies, they are able to determine where they lived as milkweed-eating caterpillars because the different types of milkweed throughout the country have unique chemical characteristics that can be tagged geographically. As a result, researchers are able to confirm some suspicions about changing migration habits, but there were also surprises. In Florida, for example, up to 48 percent of what were thought to be non-migratory Florida monarchs in a University of Florida study were proven to have originated from as far away as the Midwest and Texas, thus suggesting that almost half of the monarchs being studied had migrated from the north but for some reason remained in the state instead of moving on.

One fairly consistent result is that it seems in their travels migrating monarchs are finding some of the sites where tropical milkweed is popping up as they search for warmer climates along their paths. On the eastern coast of Texas, researchers found that as they migrate south, some of the population are mixing with resident, non-migratory monarchs, causing their OE occurrence rate to jump to 25 percent instead of the usual 9 percent found in the migrating eastern population and seemingly creeping closer to the high rates already being recorded in these non-migrating populations.

Many questions still remain about the Florida monarch and its similarities and differences when compared to the northern migrating members of the species. They are unique in that they are most abundant during the winter months when those from northern areas are hibernating. In areas of the state where milkweed grows year round and temperatures do not reach freezing, they can, and do, thrive every month of the year, compounding concerns about the higher occurrence rate of OE in Florida populations that are not feeding off of native milkweed. This population also does not seem to undergo diapause and is able to reproduce without interruption.

# PREDATORS, PARASITES, AND

## PREDATORS

Caterpillars ingest and store poisonous cardenolide compounds found in the milkweed they eat.

Milkweed sap in the eyes can cause corneal endothelial toxicity, affecting the innermost layer of the cornea and resulting in extreme pain, blurred vision, and light sensitivity.

In nature, many species have built-in mechanisms that enable them to avoid becoming prey to others. This is sometimes accomplished through a color-pattern defense (aposematic defense), where, for example, bright yellow, orange, or red color patterns warn predators of a potential toxic danger.

Milkweed, the only food eaten by monarch caterpillars, is poisonous for most vertebrates. From the time it is first hatched, the monarch caterpillar devours nothing but milkweed and immediately begins to store the cardenolide compounds that make it so poisonous. While not usually deadly, the chemical is still very toxic to many natural enemies. An attacking predator will become so sick after ingesting a monarch caterpillar that it will immediately learn to associate their bright colors with a bad experience, causing them to avoid all black-yellow-and-white caterpillars in the future.

Milkweed sap can be equally disastrous for humans. Care should always be taken to avoid transferring even a small amount of the poisonous sap to the eyes. A tiny smear inadvertently put there by an innocent sweeping motion to wipe away sweat can have extremely painful results that will most likely end with temporary vision loss, an eye patch, meds, and multiple doctor visits as a result of the corneal endothelial toxicity it causes.

Two species of birds and one mouse represent the greatest predatory threats to adult monarchs, particularly during the winter months. Both the black-backed oriole and the black-headed grosbeak have been known to eat large quantities of monarchs at overwintering sites. Neither seems to react to the toxicity, possibly because of the reduced level of toxins present in the butterflies' bodies by the time they are hibernating and far removed from their days of ingesting large amounts of milkweed leaves. It is also possible that they can simply tolerate higher levels of the cardenolides. Either way, researchers believe that these two birds account for over 60 percent of all monarch deaths during overwintering, sometimes wiping out as much as 10 percent of the entire population of a hibernating colony.

# PATHOGENS

In addition to these two birds, the black-eared mouse, which also roams the forests where overwintering monarchs are roosting, accounts for another 5 percent of annual deaths. Night feeders, they will eat living, dying, and recently killed butterflies they find on the forest floor after the birds have made their pass at the population.

Invertebrates such as ants (including fire ants in the parts of the country where they are prevalent), spiders, and wasps pose the greatest threats to milkweed-dwelling larval-stage monarchs. These predatory attacks are not limited to larvae, however, as wasps have also been found feasting on the abdomens of live adult monarchs at overwintering sites in Mexico.

## PARASITES

Parasites are small foreign organisms that complete most, if not all, of their life cycle within a host. While not all parasites actually kill their hosts, more often than not they have a negative effect on the hosts' survival and reproductive capabilities. Parasitic wasps and flies that lay their eggs directly on monarch larvae are examples of parasitic threats of this nature.

Tachinid fly lays its eggs on caterpillar's outer skin

One such parasitic fly, the *Lespesia archippivora* (*La*), is the most prevalent monarch tachinid parasitoid. The female *La* will lay its eggs on the outer skin of a host monarch caterpillar. As soon as these eggs hatch into larval form, the tiny hatchlings will then bore into the host caterpillar, where they will fully develop and then emerge as maggots during the caterpillar's late larva or early pupa stage.

Similarly, tiny *P. cassotis* wasps also parasitize monarch caterpillars, where more than 200 fully developed larvae have been known to emerge from a single pupa.

## PATHOGENS

In addition to parasites, disease-causing pathogens such as viruses and bacteria can also infect monarchs. For the most part, infectious insect parasites enter by way of oral consumption, although some do enter via pores or membrane joints. Of particular concern right now and infecting far too many monarchs across the country is a protozoan parasite called *ophryocystis elektroscirrha* (*OE*).

# Ophryocystis elektroscirrha (OE)

*Ophryocystis elektroscirrha (OE)* is not a disease but rather a spore-producing protozoan parasite that infects butterflies in the *Danaus* species group, i.e., those for whom milkweed is the host plant. This includes monarchs as well as the queen and soldier butterflies.

*OE* spores are most frequently transmitted by a caterpillar eating contaminated egg shells or milkweed leaves that it finds in its path, but there also have been incidents of spores being transmitted from an infected male to a female during mating. Monarchs infected with *OE* become carriers of large numbers of the microscopic lemon-shaped, brown or black *OE* spores, which are then left on milkweed leaves by the female as she lays her eggs or even by a male stopping to nectar. *OE* spores are carried on the outside body of an infected adult monarch making it likely that loose spores will fall from them as they fly over and near milkweed plants. They will be easily rubbed off and left behind by those stopping to nectar. In other words, they spread very easily after being introduced, and there are a lot of them.

Once inside the caterpillar's body, the spores go through additional growth stages and replicate sexually once in the pupa stage. By the time the butterfly emerges, it is covered with thousands of spores that are ready to fall off and be accidentally eaten by nearby caterpillars before it even takes flight.

*OE* will rarely kill a caterpillar, chrysalis, or adult, but it can weaken caterpillars and cripple adult butterflies. This makes sense because *OE* is a parasite that is 100 percent dependent on its host for its own survival, so killing its host would mean killing itself. Instead, heavily infected butterflies will emerge in a weakened state with severe wing deformation and will rarely be able to fly let alone survive in the wild. Those with a lower parasitic load will probably appear to be normal, but they will also be spore carriers. Sometimes when heavy *OE* contamination is present, the butterfly will crack the chrysalis open, emerge partway, then die struggling to get out. Others emerge unable to fly because they cannot expand their wings. Others simply appear weak but for no apparent reason. If any of these symptoms are visible, *OE* should be assumed.

Chrysalides with a developing heavy load of the spores will have uneven dark patches that are visible through the shell a day or two before emerging. Black patches that have a mirror image of themselves on the opposite side of the chrysalis are a good sign that the butterfly likely is unaffected, but any that appear to be singular, unmirrored dark blotches should be considered *OE* suspects. Many experts recommend euthanizing them by putting them in a plastic bag in the freezer for 48 hours.

Researchers suggest that close to 30 percent of wild monarchs in the western population have heavy *OE* spore loads, while only about 8 or 9 percent of the eastern population appear to. However, in South Florida and East Texas where monarchs

Once hailed as a godsend for restoring lost milkweed habitats, tropical milkweed (Asclepias curassavica) soon became pegged as the link to a dramatic increase in OE, especially in the southern states.

fly and lay eggs all year long, the picture is much more dismal. It is estimated that more than 70 percent carry heavy *OE* loads and that 100 percent of those in the very southern tip of the state of Florida, especially in the Miami/Dade area, are infected to some degree, from mild to heavy. The widespread availability of non-native tropical milkweed is linked to this imbalance because a 12-month growing cycle means that it does not die back in the winter months like most native milkweeds do in cooler climates, which is their built-in mechanism for killing off any of the protozoan spores dropped there by other infected monarchs.

## What can be done?

Since there is no treatment yet for already-infested butterflies, the best and only option is to try to prevent other caterpillars from eating spores that are left behind by those that are carrying them. While nothing at this point will be 100-percent effective, a few things can be done by butterfly gardeners to help:

- If possible, remove all tropical milkweed from your garden, and do not purchase any tropical milkweed in the future.

- In Florida, Texas, and other high-incidence areas, clip all milkweed back to about 4 inches every October to force a dormant period that will help to kill off any attached spores.

- Use a bleach-cleaning regimen to disinfect cages, containers, tools, milkweed leaves, and even monarch eggs. *(Instructions for this procedure follow on next page.)*

Part of any effort to help conserve the monarchs at this point must include home gardeners gaining an understanding of the risks now posed by tropical milkweed and implementing procedures that will help minimize its ill effects.

## How to Disinfect Using a Bleach Solution

Adding a bleach-cleaning regimen to raising monarchs, especially in areas where *OE* as well as NPV (discussion follows) and other bacterial infections are known to be problematic, has been shown to improve success rates.

At the very least, tropical milkweed should be clipped back to 4 inches every fall in order to emulate a forced dormant season that can aid in killing off parasitic OE spores.

Although hospital disinfectants or even using 100-percent ethanol can certainly do the job, using a mixture of 5-percent bleach to 95-percent water seems to be the best all-around and least-expensive formula. Regular household bleach is fine. Since everything from a tiny monarch egg to the entire cage or enclosure must be cleaned, two different methods of mixing the solution are provided as a matter of convenience — a smaller one-gallon size and another multi-gallon size.

## Mixture for Cleaning Eggs and Milkweed Leaves

The quickest and least-messy way to end up with one gallon of 5-percent bleach water is to:

- Begin with 1 gallon of water and use a measuring cup to remove 6.4 ounces of the water. (One gallon = 128 ounces, and 6.4 ounces is 5 percent of 128.)

- Replace the water that was removed with 6.4 ounces of bleach.

- Replace cap and gently shake to evenly distribute the bleach into the water.

### Cleaning Milkweed Leaves

*Supplies*: Prepared bleach solution, plain water, two bowls, paper towels, small plastic bags

- Fill one bowl with bleach solution and one with plain water.

- Immerse and swish leaves in the bleach solution for 10 minutes.

- Move leaves to bowl with clear water and rinse thoroughly.

- Remove and place on paper towels. Immediately cover with another clean paper towel to assure that no stray spores find their way to the disinfected leaves.

- Gently pat dry.

- Store leaves that will not be used immediately in plastic bags in refrigerator.

Disinfect with 5% Bleach / 95% Water

Place eggs (either still on a piece of leaf or removed from the leaf) in strainer before pouring the bleach solution. Remove eggs after exactly 60 seconds to avoid damaging the fragile egg.

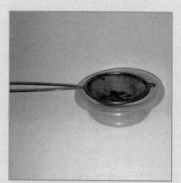

## Cleaning Monarch Eggs

This process for cleaning the tiny eggs is slightly different and requires more precision because exposure of more than one minute to the bleach solution could weaken and destroy them. The eggs can be cleaned while still on the leaves or carefully removed from the leaves.

*Supplies*: Prepared bleach solution, plain water, two bowls, small strainer, stopwatch or phone with a 60-second timer, paper towels, small plastic bags

Wrap leaf around index finger as shown and rub lightly to gently remove an egg from its leaf.

- Fill one container with clear water and set aside for the rinse phase that will follow the bleach solution.

- Place the eggs in the strainer and the strainer in the second **empty** container. The easiest and safest way is to first place the strainer in the container, then add the eggs. This will make it possible to remove all of the eggs at once when the time is up.

- Set the timer to 60 seconds and immediately pour in the prepared solution. Do not pour the liquid first and then add the eggs second because it will be impossible to accurately assure that each egg is immersed exactly one minute and no more.

- At exactly one minute, remove the strainer and place it into the container of clear water for another 60 seconds.

- Place sanitized eggs on a paper towel and cover immediately with another clean paper towel to prevent any stray spores from finding their way onto the disinfected eggs.

- Allow to dry, which should take less than an hour.

- Place eggs in a container of choice for hatching.

- Discard any unused solution as fresh solution should be made each time to avoid deterioration.

Some people are nervous the first time they try this. Consider practicing on grains of rice until you are satisfied you can do it within the designated time.

After soaking 60 seconds and then rinsing, place disinfected eggs on a piece of paper towel to dry for approximately 1 hour.

## Mixture for Cleaning Cages, Tools, and Larger Items

Larger items obviously require far more solution as it is imperative that everything be completely immersed if the procedure is to be effective. Larger containers such as plastic laundry bins can be picked up inexpensively at most discount stores. Keeping the same proportions to achieve the 5-percent bleach target, mix 9-1/2 gallons of plain water with each 1/2 gallon of bleach. Working outside is suggested but not required as the bleach can be both messy and cause some damage to clothing and surrounding surfaces if care is not taken.

*Supplies*: Prepared bleach solution, plain water, two large containers that will accommodate enough water to cover the entire cage or larger items to be disinfected, stick or stirrer, rubber gloves, yardwork clothing

- Fill both bins with water deep enough to cover the largest item. Add bleach (last) to one of the bins. The second bin will be used for rinsing. Stir gently to be sure bleach is evenly distributed.

- Insert items to be disinfected, assuring that everything is fully covered with the solution. If necessary, use a stick to agitate the water during the process. Sometimes a heavier piece of wood or other item is helpful to hold a cage under water that keeps floating to the surface.

- Soak for 10 minutes then remove.

- Rinse well in another tub of clear water, approximately 10 minutes.

- Allow to completely dry before using. Sunlight is recommended but not necessary.

- Discard remaining solution as it will weaken after a short period of time, but be careful not to spill on clothing or surrounding area.

## How to Check Adult Monarchs for the Presence of *OE*

Before releasing newly emerged butterflies, it is easy to check them for *OE* spores. Spores are microscopic in size and not visible by the naked eye. A simple pocket microscope that can magnify up to 120X can be purchased online for less than $20. To obtain the necessary spore sample, simply hold the butterfly with wings pinched together and abdomen and thorax visible. Use a piece ordinary office tape (not magic tape) wrapped so the sticky side is out and gently press it to the butterfly's abdomen. Place on an index card, and view under the microscope. The spores are easy to see against the wing scales that will also be present.

60-120X LED Lighted Pocket Microscope

Spore Specimen on Scotch Tape

Magnification of Spore Specimen

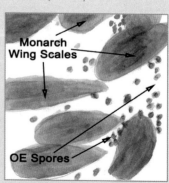

Monarch Wing Scales

OE Spores

## Nuclear Polyhedrosis Virus (NPV)

Also referred to as "Melt," "Wilt," and "Black Death," the nuclear polyhedrosis virus (NPV) is always fatal and is not limited to just milkweed-eating butterflies such as the monarchs. It is therefore important to recognize the signs and to understand what needs to be done immediately to minimize the damage the virus can cause.

Diseased caterpillars will usually crawl to the top of their container, hang in an inverted "V," and then die — mushy, wet, and dripping black fluid. Prior to this, they will have been sluggish, uninterested in eating, and rather oily looking. They also may be regurgitating whatever they try to eat.

Between their regurgitation and the fluid that drips from their bodies after they have died, caterpillars stricken with NPV also end up spreading the dripping virus all over their host plants and in the direct path of other caterpillars. In the end, it will kill all of them. Nectaring butterflies may also track remnants of the killer virus to other host plants as they go from plant to plant.

Infected caterpillars, if they are still alive, should be humanely euthanized by placing them in the freezer in a sealed plastic bag for 48 hours. Before discarding, a small amount of bleach should be poured into the bag and then resealed.

Equally important, the same disinfecting routine should be followed that was described for dealing with *OE*. The assumption should be made that if one caterpillar has NPV, they all most likely will have it. It is critically important that any of the dripping, virus-packed fluid be located and bleach cleaned so that other caterpillars do not become sick.

**WILT, MELT, BLACK DEATH:** infected caterpillar will eventually deteriorate into black, drippy goo.

- Quarantine all remaining caterpillars so that they can be observed to determine whether they have also been infected.

- Discard any leaves that may still be in the containers.

- Follow the same procedures described previously to disinfect all containers, tools, and cages in 5-percent bleach solution for at least 10 minutes.

- Disinfect and rinse any plants or leaves that may have been infected.

Together with *OE*, the nuclear polyhedrosis virus (NPV) and bacterial infections represent the three greatest threats to monarchs besides predators.

# MALE OR FEMALE?

It is not always easy to differentiate between male or female butterflies in general because the clues vary and are different from species to species. In many species, there is no obvious difference between the two; in others, there are subtle differences that make it much easier to figure out which is which. For example, sometimes size tells the story. When this is the case, the male tends to be smaller but more vibrantly colored, while the female, who needs more room to carry her eggs, may be a bit larger and is usually not as colorful. Sometimes it is behavior that provides the clues as it will be the female flitting from plant to plant as she deposits her eggs on the preferred host plant for her species. The males, on the other hand, will be the ones chasing the females, puddling (using their proboscis to drink up liquid nutrients), and generally trying to protect their turf.

Fortunately, monarchs are one species that does provide distinctly unique visible clues that make differentiation much easier once you know what to look for. In fact, it is possible to determine the sex of the monarch in both its chrysalis and adult form.

**Chrysalis:** A close look at a newly formed chrysalis reveals a small black stem at the top that is the point of attachment to the surface. This is called the cremaster. Just beneath the cremaster are two rows of paired black dots. It is possible to determine the gender of the monarch butterfly that will emerge in a week or two by looking closely at this formation. If a vertical line can be seen in the segment just below the paired dots, the butterfly is female. If the area below the dots is smooth and without this vertical line, it is a male.

**Adult Butterfly:** Male monarchs have scent glands that are located at the base of each hindwing. At a quick glance, these glands look like smudges that seem to be kind of bleeding out from the vein line into a small, black circle. The female will not have the dark smudges on her wings, and veins in these hindwings also tend to be darker in the female than the male.

FEMALE

Line Below Dots

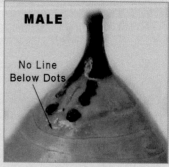

MALE

No Line Below Dots

FEMALE

Thicker Veins

Visible Scent Glands

MALE

# BUTTERFLY OR MOTH?

Although all butterflies and moths belong to the insect family of Lepidoptera, there are several very distinct differences in appearance and behavior that differentiate them.

• Moths have plump, fuzzy bodies, whereas butterfly bodies are smooth and slender.

• Butterflies are active during the day and dormant at night, while moths prefer nighttime for their activities.

• Moths are typically dull in color as nature provides them with natural camouflage for their evening activities. Butterflies, on the other hand, are often, although not always, more colorful to make them more visible in the light of day.

• When perched, butterflies hold their wings upward; moths usually hold theirs horizontally at their sides.

• Moth wings are more scaly than butterfly wings.

• Butterfly pupa develop inside a shell-like chrysalis that is usually hung by a silken thread, whereas the moth is wrapped in a silk-like cocoon that is often buried beneath leaves or soil.

• Moth antennae are feathery or thin; butterfly antennae have small, rounded clubs at the very end.

• Moth antennae are wider on the male than on the female because they use them to track the scent-producing female. It is the reverse with butterflies: males produce the scent to attract the females.

# MONARCH OR QUEEN?

The queen butterfly is the monarch's closest relative and shares its dependency on milkweed as the sole host plant. Both belong to the *Danaus* genus, with the queen's scientific name being *Danaus gilippus* and the monarch's *Danaus plexippus*. Other distinguishing features include:

**MONARCH**

**QUEEN**

• The term "queen" does not mean there are no males. There are both male and female queen butterflies, and the males can be distinguished from the females by scent glands that are similar to those of the monarch male.

• The ventral (underside) wings are similar on both, but the monarch's dorsal (topside) wings are bright orange with black veins separating each cell while the queen's orange is more muted and without the vein separators.

• Queens have white dots distributed throughout their orange wings while the monarchs' white markings are only on the black areas.

• The larvae of both have stripes of white, black, and yellow but their patterns are different.

• Monarch larvae have filaments in the head and tail areas only while queens have an additional set of filaments halfway between the front and back sets.

• Monarch abdomens are black and queens' are brown.

# CONSERVATION

## The Problem

People are drawn to learning about and raising monarchs for a number of reasons, not the least of which is the fascination with experiencing their beauty and unique life cycle. Unfortunately, however, monarchs have been making the headlines in recent years as researchers suggest that there is a risk that the entire species could be eradicated unless immediate and dramatic efforts are made to save the monarch.

The National Wildlife Federation estimates that since 1990, the monarch population in North America has declined by approximately 90 percent. This startling revelation is attributed to loss of habitat brought on by an increase in developers constructing buildings on fields where milkweed was once abundant along with an increase in the use of butterfly- and caterpillar-killing pesticides and herbicides by farmers in the Midwest. In urban, suburban, rural, and industrialized settings across the country, milkweeds — some of which are actually beautiful flowering plants — have been perceived to be noxious weeds and completely eradicated. This is further complicated by the fact that although monarch populations have historically been known to fluctuate widely from year to year following extraordinary natural occurrences like hurricanes, earthquakes, droughts, or most recently the horrific flooding that killed livestock and ruined crops in 2019, scientists now fear that these types of weather-related, habitat-destroying events are becoming the norm. The combined impact of all of these factors is causing a disruption in the reproductive patterns of migrating monarch generations, the result of which is a monarch population that is no longer able to reproduce at acceptable rates.

A severely declining monarch population could also have a very profound and damaging effect on the ecosystem and on other species along the food chain, including humans. In nature, pollination is primarily provided by pollinators: bees, wasps, moths, flies, beetles, and butterflies. Monarchs are pollinators. A pollinator, as defined by Northwestern University, is

**POLLINATOR:** an animal that causes plants to make fruit or seeds. They do this by moving pollen from one part of the flower of a plant to another part. This pollen then fertilizes the plant.

*Bumblebee & Monarch Co-Pollinators*
*Image: US Fish and Wildlife Service*

"an animal that causes plants to make fruit or seeds. They do this by moving pollen from one part of the flower of a plant to another part. This pollen then fertilizes the plant." Pollination is an essential ecological function that is necessary for the survival of the human race through the role it plays in helping to keep earth's ecosystems in balance.

Of the 1,300 to 1,400 crop plants in the world — i.e., those that produce all of the food, medicines, and other plant-based products — more than 75 percent depend on animals for pollination. According to the USDA, more than 150 food crops in the US, including almost all fruit and grain crops, depend on pollinators. Pollinator researcher Claire Kremen at the University of California summarized the important role played by pollinators in her observation that, "There's a widely stated phrase in agriculture that you can thank a pollinator for one out of three bites of food you eat."

As pollinators, monarchs contribute to the necessary task of pollinating as they flutter from flower to flower transporting tiny specs of yellow pollen along the way, especially during migration. A significant reduction in their numbers could lead to a severe reduction in the diversity and quantity of these flowering plants. In turn, the impact on the food chain down the line could be exponential as fewer monarchs pollinating fewer plants will result in fewer insects being able to find their preferred food sources. Of course, this will then trickle down to the bird population being affected when they, too, become unable to find adequate numbers of the insects they need to survive. This snowballing effect will move along the food chain affecting larger predators that are in need of birds for their survival, until it eventually touches on the human food supply.

## Programs, Resources, and Available Help

In the US there is already a massive effort to provide and restore habitat for monarchs through a variety of programs, agencies, and organizations, public, private, and governmental:

• In response to the many issues that are now tied either directly or indirectly to the monarch's diminishing numbers, the US Fish and Wildlife Service along with the Department of Agriculture's Natural Resources Conservation Service have put in place initiatives for land to be set aside for habitats designed to increase milkweed growth, especially in ten Midwestern and Plains states where there is the greatest need. In addition, both the Mexican and the Canadian governments are working to institute similar programs in their countries. In Mexico, for example, where deforestation has resulted in the loss of overwintering habitats for monarchs that come from as far away as Canada, monarch reserves have been established to protect their guests.

• The National Wildlife Federation and the US Fish and Wildlife Service are working together to create a coalition of agricultural and highway transportation leaders to spearhead a program in support of planting milkweed and nectar plants on roadsides along the migratory flyways and breeding grounds in key Midwestern and Texas corridors.

• A number of government agencies, non-profits, corporations and individuals have joined forces to coordinate efforts aimed at improving, restoring, and even creating new habitats for the flailing monarch population. One such organization is the Monarch Joint Venture, which is a partnership of federal and state agencies, non-governmental organizations, businesses, and academic entities working together to protect the monarch migration across the US. Partnering organizations are made up of experts in monarch conservation and education whose ultimate goal is to conserve monarch migration.

• There are a number of tagging studies underway across the country where designated butterflies are tagged and numbered so that their progress can be monitored and logged in along the way as sightings are reported.

• Monarch Watch's Monarch Waystation Program provides information for individuals to set up oasis-like monarch waystations along the migratory path that are planted with nectar-filled flowering plants to provide nutrition for the migrating masses.

## How Individuals Can Make a Difference

It follows, therefore, that there has never been a greater need for individual involvement in helping to reverse the alarming trend before it is too late. There are a number of ways to individually contribute to these efforts:

• Raise and release home-grown butterflies and in so doing help increase the overall monarch population, of which it is estimated that only 1 to 5 percent actually survive and grow to adulthood in the wild.

• Create a monarch habitat by planting a butterfly garden populated with native milkweed as well as other native wildflowers that are known to attract butterflies in your area. Ask friends, neighbors, schools, and communities to do the same.

• Discontinue the use of pesticides in your own yard,

*Monarch Watch Waystation*

THREATENED SPECIES: any species that is likely to become an endangered species within the foreseeable future throughout all or a significant portion of its range. *(US Fish and Wildlife Service)*

Image: USFWS / NCTC Library

and pass the word on to everyone you know. Organic products are inexpensive and readily available.

• Help save the grasslands, which is a critical need because they provide both host and nectar plants.

• Help cut back on deforestation that is ruining overwintering sites by monitoring your own consumption of wood and paper products.

• Become an advocate in your community: share information, advocate for farming practices that do not eradicate milkweed, talk to property managers and local government about reducing mowing, especially in late summer when the need for nectar plants is greatest.

• Become a citizen scientist and participate in programs that encourage reporting monarch observations, which are then compiled together with other data collected by scientists studying monarch behavior.

## What Will the Future Hold?

The xerces blue butterfly, once abundant near San Francisco, was the first North American butterfly to be declared extinct after urbanization destroyed its natural habitat. Last seen around 1941 or 1942, loss of its host plant, the lotus, has been cited as the primary reason for its disappearance.

While the monarch's current crisis is not yet to a point where it should be officially designated threatened or endangered, there are lessons to be learned from past mistakes that led to the extinction of the xerces. Furthermore, at the time of this writing, in the US alone there are at least 12 different butterfly species that are currently designated either threatened or endangered. While not there yet, the monarch is inching dangerously close to such a designation.

Fortunately, it is not too late. With the increased attention being directed toward the monarch's plunging population in the last 20 years, more and more people are becoming aware of its plight. Awareness is a crucial first step that will hopefully lead to increased efforts to stop the nosedive and turn things around.

# MILKWEED

Milkweed is an indispensable part of the monarch life cycle. The female needs it for her eggs. The hatchlings must eat it to survive. Adult monarchs need its nectar, especially when fall approaches and migration draws near. The monarch's very existence depends on the availability of milkweed; but loss of habitat, especially naturally growing native milkweed, has been tied very closely to the 90-percent decrease in the monarch population over the last 20 years. Milkweed-filled meadowlands, once abundant across the entire country, are disappearing as new housing developments pop up, farming practices change, and unusual weather events flood areas never before under water. Researchers, not-for-profit organizations, and even the US Fish and Wildlife Service continue to evaluate the problem with an eye toward coming up with some kind of a plan to help turn this fast-moving tragedy around before it is too late.

That being said, there has been a call to arms of sorts for people across the country to pitch in by including milkweed in their personal landscaping plans. Butterfly gardens have become very popular, and there is an increased surge in demand for milkweed plants to be front and center in private gardens. In order to fully maximize any efforts that might be put forth in such an endeavor, there are some specific things to keep in mind when considering what to include:

## What to plant?

Plant milkweed species that are native to your geographic area only. This might require a little research, but it is critical to try to emulate nature by using the kind of plants that have grown or do grow naturally in the area. There are more than 70 species of milkweed native to the US, 30 of which are known to be monarch host plants. All milkweed belong to the genus *Asclepias,* so this will always be the first part in their two-part scientific name. Several are endangered, rare, and/or difficult to find. Monarch Joint Venture (www.monarchjointventure.org) recommends the following by region:

### Northeast Region

*[Connecticut, Delaware, Illinois, Indiana, Iowa, Kansas (Eastern), Kentucky, Maine, Maryland, Massachusetts, Michigan, Minnesota, Missouri, N. Dakota (Eastern), Nebraska (Eastern), New Hampshire, New Jersey, New York, Ohio, Pennsylvania, Rhode Island, S. Dakota (Eastern), Vermont, Virginia, W. Virginia, Washington DC, Wisconsin]*

Common Milkweed (*Asclepias syriaca*) — Well-drained soils
Swamp Milkweed (*Asclepias incarnata*) — Damp, marshy areas
Butterfly Weed (*Asclepias tuberosa*) — Well-drained soils
Whorled Milkweed (*Asclepias verticillata*) — Prairies and open areas
Poke Milkweed (*Asclepias exaltata*) — Woodland areas *(except in Nebraska, Kansas, Missouri, North & South Dakota)*

## South Central Region

*[Texas and Oklahoma excluding Panhandle]*

Green Antelope Horn Milkweed (*Asclepias viridis*) — Dry areas and prairies. (Also known as Green Milkweed)
Antelope Horns Milkweed (*Asclepias asperula*) — Desert and sandy areas
Zizotes Milkweed (*Asclepias oenotheroides*) — Sandy / rocky prairies and fields

## Southeast Region

*[Alabama, Arkansas, Florida, Georgia, Louisiana, Mississippi, N. Carolina, S. Carolina, Tennessee]*

Butterfly Weed (*Asclepias tuberosa*) — Well-drained soils
Whorled Milkweed (*Asclepias verticillata*) — Prairies and open areas
White Milkweed (*Asclepias variegata*) — Thickets and woodlands
Aquatic Milkweed (*Asclepias perennis*) — Hydrated soils
Sandhill / Pinewoods Milkweed (*Asclepias humistrata*) — Dry, sandy areas and soils; appropriate for some regions of Florida
Common Milkweed (*Asclepias syriaca*) and Swamp Milkweed (*Asclepias incarnata*) are native to Florida and other parts of this region

## Western Region

*[Colorado, Idaho, Kansas (Western), Montana, N. Dakota (Western), Nebraska (Western), Nevada, New Mexico, Oklahoma (Panhandle), Oregon, S. Dakota (Western), Utah, Washington, Wyoming]*

Mexican Whorled Milkweed (*Asclepias fascicularis*) — Dry climates and plains, except in Colorado, Utah, New Mexico, and Arizona
Showy Milkweed (*Asclepias speciosa*) — Savannahs and prairies

## Arizona Region

Butterfly Weed (*Asclepias tuberosa*) — Well-drained soils
Antelope Horns Milkweed (*Asclepias asperula*) — Desert and sandy areas
Rush Milkweed (*Asclepias subulata*) — Desert areas
Arizona Milkweed (*Asclepias angustifolia*) — Riparian areas and canyons

## California Region

Mexican Whorled Milkweed (*Asclepias fascicularis*) — Dry climates and plains
Showy Milkweed (*Asclepias speciosa*) — Savannahs and prairies
Desert Milkweed (*Asclepias erosa*) — Desert regions
California Milkweed (*Asclepias californica*) — Grassy areas
Heartleaf Milkweed (*Asclepias cordifolia*) — Rocky slopes
Wooly Milkweed (*Asclepias vestita*) — Dry deserts and plains
Wooly Pod Milkweed (*Asclepias eriocarpa*) — Clay soils and dry areas

## Why are native plants necessary?

Native plants are recommended for a number of reasons. They are hardy, designed by nature to live in that area, and as a result will also require less maintenance. More important, however, are the problems that may result when non-native species are introduced into an area that is not natural to them. This has especially become a problem in the southern US with the introduction of tropical milkweed (*Asclepias curassavica*). Native milkweed species in northern states for the most part are subject to the effects of the seasons. That is, when cold weather sets in during winter, native milkweed will lose its leaves, die, and then return in the spring. This cycle does not occur with non-native tropical milkweed. This non-native milkweed does not experience a winter season, and therefore it keeps growing 12 months a year without stop. Without a winter season to shut things down, any parasites attached to the plant will continue to thrive, uninterrupted. Originally hailed as a lifesaver for the declining monarch populations, research now indicates that tropical milkweed may be linked to extraordinarily high levels of *OE* now being detected on most wild-growing milkweed plants found especially in South Florida and East Texas. Availability of milkweed 24/7 also causes butterflies passing through the area on their way south to shorten their migration and consequently increase their exposure to *OE*.

## Is native milkweed more difficult to find?

More and more local nurseries are becoming involved in the nationwide efforts to save the monarch. As a result, many are increasingly conscious about finding milkweed that is native to their area so they should be an initial source. It is also always a good idea to have a discussion about their herbicide and pesticide policy and whether plants have been sprayed. A directory of plant vendors that sell native milkweed plants and seeds can be found at plantmilkweed.org. There is also a link to the Xerces Society's Milkweed Seed Finder tool.

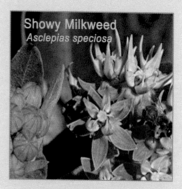

Showy Milkweed
*Asclepias speciosa*

Antelope Horn Milkweed
*Asclepias asperula*

Desert Milkweed
*Asclepias erosa*

Milkweed Going to Seed
*Image: NPS Yosemite*

Aquatic Milkweed
*Asclepias perennis*

Swamp Milkweed
*Asclepias incarnata*

Butterfly Weed
*Asclepias tuberosa*

Whorled Milkweed
*Asclepias verticillata*

## Should seeds or plants be used?

This decision can be left to personal preference. Purchasing potted plants is obviously an easier way to get a jumpstart if seeds were not planted at the end of the previous season or perennial plants are not already established in the ground from previous seasons. If seeds are planted, remember that most milkweed species are perennials. Seeds must therefore be planted sometime in the previous fall. As deciduous perennials, the typical US native milkweed will flower late spring to the end of summer. They will go to seed and die back to the ground as their season ends and will remain dormant throughout the winter until they re-appear from their already-established root system the following spring.

The National Wildlife Federation identified the following as the 12 best native milkweed species for North American monarchs. The previous list can also be compared to determine appropriateness for a given geographic area:

- Common Milkweed
- Butterfly Weed
- Swamp Milkweed
- Antelope Horn
- Purple Milkweed
- Showy Milkweed
- California Milkweed
- White Milkweed
- Whorled Milkweed
- Mexican Whorled Milkweed
- Desert Milkweed
- Green Milkweed

## Is it worth It?

*No milkweed* means *no monarchs*, it's as simple as that. The best way to help the declining population is for everyone to pitch in wherever possible. Besides the enjoyment gained from seeing all of the butterflies passing through whether they are headed north or south, there is real pleasure in the beauty all of the flowers will also add to any landscape.

NOTEWORTHY: Although this has already been mentioned once, it is important enough to merit emphasis: Corneal endothelial toxicity is real. Always take care to keep milkweed sap away from the eyes. Even a small drop can result in blurred vision and even blindness for several weeks, and it is very painful.

# PLANTING A GARDEN

As noted in earlier chapters, a number of federal and state agencies, private non-profits, non-governmental programs, and academic groups have recognized the urgency of the monarch's fragile status, and in response they have stepped forward to create a variety of programs and aid groups aimed at the conservation of monarch habitats. In that vein, a common question that often comes their way is, "What can we do to help?"

"Plant a butterfly garden. Plant native milkweed. Help replace lost habitats."

Whether starting a new garden from scratch or upgrading an existing one to make it appealing to monarchs, several key steps should be taken to assure a favorable outcome, beginning with pinpointing how you envision the end product.

"I want a garden that contributes to the movement to replace lost monarch habitats."

Great, goal identified. Let's begin!

## Have a Plan

The ideal habitat must support visiting monarchs throughout all four of their life-cycle stages — egg, larva, pupa, and adult — preferably using plants that are native to the geographical area or that would have grown there had they not been eliminated by developers or farmers along the way:

• The female monarch will need both milkweed on which to lay her eggs and nectar plants for her own nourishment, as will her male counterpart.

• The hatchlings that will emerge from the eggs deposited on the milkweed by the female will continue to need milkweed as their sole source of nourishment until they are ready to pupate, when all eating will be suspended.

• No food sources are necessary when in chrysalis form, but the adult butterfly that emerges will immediately seek flowering plants for nectar.

In essence, any garden intended to support monarchs must contain ample and varied amounts of both milkweed and nectar-rich flowering plants. The garden does not necessarily need to be big to be effective. Rather, it must provide a balance of host and nectar plants that offer a one-stop variety of resources to your monarch visitors at any stage of their life cycle.

As you plan, it can be helpful to have an idea of when monarchs typically come through your area as that will vary from region to region. The Journey North website at journeynorth.org posts sighting maps for the current year as well as historical information about prior years and is a great way to get a general idea of when a nectaring mass may be headed your way. Your garden habitat must be able to accommodate the early-summer reproducing monarchs as well as the late-season nectar-seeking monarchs that need an extra boost for their trip south.

## What to Include

Native milkweed as well as native flowering plants are always preferable since they are best adapted to local conditions and usually require less maintenance. Nature put them there because that was the best place for them to survive and thrive.

**Milkweed.** A well-balanced garden should always include three or four types of milkweed to provide both variety as well as staggered blooming cycles. Plant in groups of six to eight of the same type, preferably native species. There can never be too much milkweed because of the dual role it plays as both a host and a nectar plant. Caterpillars need to eat milkweed to survive, and adult monarchs, along with many other butterflies and pollinators, need the milkweed flowers for their nectar. It should be the central plant in the garden.

Non-native varieties should be avoided. Especially important in southern states in particular is the need to resist the temptation to buy tropical milkweed (Asclepias curssavica). This non-native milkweed is abundant, readily available, and has attractive flowers that admittedly can really dress up a garden. Unfortunately, tropical milkweed is also the cause of much concern among scientists, who suspect that its constant blooming and widespread availability have made it too easy for this non-native species to entice migrating monarchs into remaining in Florida for longer than they naturally would have had it not been so accessible. Its constant growing cycle does not naturally include a dormant period to kill off any parasites — OE in particular — and consequently puts the visiting monarchs at increased risk.

*(Refer to the previous chapter on milkweed to determine which types of milkweed are native to your area. Many local nurseries now try to stock native species of live plants, while seeds for native milkweed varieties can also be found online.)*

**Nectar plants.** Like milkweed, nectar plants must also serve a dual role. In the early summer months, their presence in the garden habitat is essential for feeding the reproducing generations. Early-blooming native and non-native plants are needed at the beginning of the summer to provide nourishment to female monarchs on the hunt for milkweed on which to deposit their eggs. Their male counterparts will also be in the area seeking nectar.

The garden should have as many native plants as possible, including perennials, as they will be the ones that will come up automatically each spring. During the growing season, butterflies will be attracted by an array of colorful plants that bloom at different times. These early-blooming plants are critical for attracting the new females who have or will soon have the task of laying hundreds of eggs.

Very important but often overlooked in the excitement of spring planting is the fact that the monarchs' feeding needs will change as summer draws to an end and fall approaches. The generation of butterflies likely to visit the garden at this point will not be there to lay eggs. Rather, they will be those needing to tank up on extra nectar in preparation for the long flight to their overwintering sites. Therefore, your selection of flowering plants must also include those that are known to be late bloomers. In fact, recent research indicates that a decrease in availability of end-of-season nectar plants may play as big of a role as milkweed does in the declining monarch population. In many parts of the country, goldenrods are excellent late bloomers that can provide excellent nectar well into late fall.

What to plant, of course, may vary from region to region. It is important to research your own area to be sure that late bloomers are included in your plant purchases. Select plants that will welcome new visitors, and do not make the mistake of trying to cut corners with these late-blooming nectar plants thinking that fewer will be needed since the end of the growing season is near. Instead, think in terms of your garden hosting one of the giant migrating flocks roosting and passing through on their way south. They will need nourishment, water, and a safe haven for the night.

Establish a relationship with a nursery that sells native plants. Most nurseries will have this information posted, but do not be afraid to ask if you are not sure. It is also important to find out their spraying policy and whether pesticides are routinely used.

## The Set-Up

- Select a location that will get at least six hours of direct sunlight per day. Butterflies need the sun's energy for warmth, and most nectar plants and milkweed do best in sunlight anyway. Low-clay soil with good drainage is suggested to avoid root rot.

- Scatter a few large, flat rocks throughout for perching butterflies to bask in the heat of the sun. Dark-colored stones will hold more heat as the weather cools.

- If possible, locate the garden in an area where a fence or other natural structure can cut off some of the wind and stormy weather that will come from time to time. Strategically positioned, these structures will also offer fully mature caterpillars a safe place to pupate.

- Planting milkweed as well as nectar plants close together will help to create a sheltered area that will also provide protection to monarchs, other butterflies, bees, and pollinators.

- Arrange plants in a pleasing pattern, grouping them by color and putting the lower ones in front. Butterflies especially like large splashes of loud colors — red, orange, yellow, and purple. Consequently, they tend to choose brightly colored wildflowers that grow in clusters and stay open during the warmth of the day so that they can easily land on them. Planting in blocks of six to eight of each species and color is a good way to accomplish this. Avoid hybrids if possible as they generally do not have much nectar, and single-flower plants are always preferrable.

Another way to contribute to the monarch conservation movement is to create and register your garden as a Monarch Waystation at www.monarchwatch.org/waystations/, where guidance is provided and all Certified Waystations are assigned a unique number and listed on their interactive online directory and map.

The vastness of the North American continent precludes there being any kind of optimal "one-size-fits-all" garden plan, but the USDA does provide a Plant Hardiness Zone Map at https://planthardiness.ars.usda.gov/PHZMWeb/ to help determine which plants are best for any given area. There are also several plants that are garden favorites and known to do well in many geographic areas:

**Milkweed Plants** (all with differing blooming cycles)
**Swamp Milkweed** (*Asclepias incarnata*): Pretty pink flowers and great fragrance; native to most of the US and parts of Canada.
**Showy Milkweed** (*Asclepias speciosa*): Pink flowers with white centers; native to western US and parts of Canada.
**Butterfly Weed** (*Asclepias tuberosa*): Native throughout most of North America; great nectar but possibly avoided by some female monarchs because of toughness of the leaves.

**Nectar Plants**
**Joe Pye Weed** (*Eutrochium*): Perennial, native in many areas, pink blooms and late bloomer.
**Mexican Sunflower** (*Tithphia rotundifolia*): Popular with monarchs across North America.
**Butterfly Bushes** (*Baddleia davidii*): Long blooming cycle attracts monarchs, hummingbirds, and many other butterflies. Considered invasive in some western states. Two derivations are less invasive, and both attract monarchs: **Buddleia Buzz Butterfly Bush** and **Miss Molly Butterfly Bush**.
***Lantana Camara***: Perennial in the South; annual in the North. Blooms all summer and attracts lots of butterflies and other pollinators. Wide variety of colors.
**Meadow Blazing Star** (*Liatris ligulistylis*): Top nectar monarch attractor and late bloomer. Plant at least 10.
**Goldenrod:** Late bloomer, well into the fall. Loved by migrating monarchs.
**Annual Nectar Plants** (bloom quickly and need to be replanted each year): Zinnias, marigolds
**Perennial Nectar Plants** (longer to root; return year after year): Black-eyed Susan, hollyhock, *Echinacea*

Monarchs need places to roost, rest, nectar, and find water during their long migration.

Monarchs are drawn to loud splashes of color arranged in groups of each color.

Image: Jessica Boiser, USFWS

# RAISING MONARCHS AND . . .

## Two Sides to Every Coin

There is some debate among researchers and scientists as to the wisdom of encouraging private individuals to independently raise and release monarchs. In areas like South Florida and East Texas in particular where some level of *OE* can be detected in nearly 100 percent of the monarchs tested, some believe that independent monarch breeding has the potential for further devastation of the species. The primary concern is the belief that unmonitored and unmanaged breeding may, in fact, add to the monarchs' problems instead of helping by unwittingly facilitating an even deeper spread of the *OE* parasites into the wild population.

There is some concern that novices, who are unfamiliar with and/or unconcerned about the disinfecting and *OE*-checking protocols, are not buying into the absolute necessity of the precautions and in essence end up working against any progress being made toward minimizing the spread, either knowingly or unknowingly. Although the enthusiasm and desire to help are understood, too many variables are now being thrown into the paths of researchers as they attempt to collect data and study the best way to help the species before it is too late. This group would prefer for public involvement to be directed toward creating new habitats, improving existing ones, and participating in and spearheading citizen-scientist and educational activities.

The other side of this conversation is that even conceding there may be some truth in the arguments, at this point there is already too much public interest and participation to even try to curtail home breeding, if there even could be a viable way to do so. In fact, one would have to argue that in many cases it is *because of* opportunities for personalized hands-on experiences with monarchs that individuals first learn to appreciate and be excited about them in the first place. Without an encounter of some sort, many people would never have become involved with monarch conservation at all, mostly because they

CITIZEN SCIENTIST: an individual who voluntarily contributes his or her time, effort, and resources toward scientific research either in collaboration with professional scientists or alone.
*https://www.citizenscience.org/*

Larger caterpillars will devour entire leaves, including any eggs that happen to be in their way.

# CONTINUING THE JOURNEY

would have had little occasion to even be exposed to the species' pending problems.

Taking both positions into account, the obvious compromise is education, moderation, and diligent *OE* monitoring by any and all parties involved. An increased emphasis on education and better public awareness of the monarch's plight must be accompanied by information that also familiarizes home breeders with responsible practices they can put into place to at least contribute to minimizing the current epidemic spread of *OE*. Most people who are already interested enough to bother to raise butterflies at all will likely be receptive to learning any necessary precautions they should be taking that will benefit their own efforts.

At present, in addition to the issues of habitat loss, use of herbicides and pesticides, and climate change, the recent surge in the occurrence of *OE* is certainly cause for concern. Its suspected link to non-native tropical milkweed and the potential ultimate impact on the future migratory behavior of the entire species are significantly important details about raising monarchs that must be embraced by anyone having any contact with monarchs if any progress is to be made in curtailing the spread of this pathogen.

Implementing a few preventive practices can have a big impact on the success rates realized by anyone trying to raise and release monarchs from home within the confines of managing their breeding routines around any *OE* threats. Home breeders are encouraged to:

> • Curtail the urge to produce and release unusually large quantities of monarchs, especially in areas where the occurrence of *OE* is particularly high. Raising and releasing smaller quantities related to research, citizen science, education, and just the pure joy and pleasure of doing so is perfectly acceptable and in its own way contributes to the overall conservation of the species.

> • Refrain from buying or selling monarch eggs outside of your geographic area. Such practices contribute to the spread of *OE*.

| OE MINIMIZATION CHECKLIST |
| --- |
| ☑ No massive breeding |
| ☑ No eggs from outside geographic area |
| ☑ Separate large cats from eggs |
| ☑ Separate large cats from smaller cats |
| ☑ No cats in cage with chrysalides |
| ☑ Bleach-cleaning / disinfecting routine |
| ☑ Routinely test for OE |
| ☑ Plant native milkweed only |
| ☑ Avoid tropical milkweed |
| ☑ Clip milkweed to 4" every October |
| ☑ Handle cats as little as possible |
| ☑ Isolate black and sick-looking cats |

• Do not keep full-grown caterpillars in the same enclosure as the smaller ones, and definitely do not keep any caterpillars of any size in the same container as a chrysalis. Emerging butterflies could be infected with *OE* and will immediately begin to shed spores that will be present on the outside of their bodies. Any caterpillars grazing on nearby milkweed leaves when they eclose will stand the risk of ingesting spores and thereby also becoming infected.

• Implement a bleach-cleaning and disinfecting regimen as previously described that involves routinely cleaning all cages, tools, countertops, milkweed leaves, and eggs brought in from the wild.

• Learn how to test each adult monarch for the presence of *OE* spores before releasing them into the wild.

• Plant only native milkweed, and try to avoid tropical milkweed. In warm climates, at the very least be sure to cut all milkweed back to approximately 4 inches every October.

• Handle caterpillars as little as possible, and immediately remove and isolate any that are turning black or appear to be sick or sluggish.

Oftentimes part of the joy of raising butterflies is simply being able to help others learn about them too, but sharing only healthy monarchs will help to minimize further spread of *OE* and other diseases. The best way to accomplish this is to raise several generations in captivity, consistently disinfecting and checking for spores from each generation so that the healthiest ones can be mated. When the infection level of those being born in captivity reaches 5 percent (1 infected butterfly out of every 100 tested), it is safe to assume that the next generation they produce can be shared with others.

As a South Floridian myself, I am naturally quite concerned about the escalated level of the infection being found in my state and the threat that it poses to the survival of this beloved species. I am also very puzzled, however, by the lack of public knowledge about this phenomenon especially here in Florida. I have been raising monarchs in my yard and making butterfly cages for nearly 20 years, and I have to admit that I do not recall ever seeing or hearing anything about *OE* in my everyday life. To my knowledge, there is no obvious discussion of it at any of the various nature walks or butterfly gardens I have recently visited. I am only aware of the problem because I have actively sought more in-depth information about monarchs due to personal interest and basically only accidentally ran across it. Based on conversations I have had, I am fairly certain that the average person picking up a few tropical milkweed plants at a local nursery or discount store because they enjoy having butterflies in their yard has absolutely no idea about the current peril of the monarch. Even within several butterfly-related discussion groups, awareness is surprisingly low. If the groups are not hearing much or anything about it "on the streets," so to speak, it is inconceivable to think that many others are either.

In spite of this, if asked, most people would be able to identify a monarch if challenged to do so, and most would probably also not want to see it become extinct. Just like many years ago when the iconic figure of Smokey the Bear was used successfully to increase awareness of forest fires through the playing of his "Only you can prevent forest fires" television messages over and over again, some type of high-profile awareness campaign might be the best recourse to help get the word out and educate the public while there is still time.

## Finding Eggs and Beginning Your Own Journey

Monarch butterflies are undoubtedly the most recognizable butterflies in North America. They are the source of much intrigue and wonder for anyone from the casual observer all the way up to the research scientist, resulting in countless books and other printed material that are just as broad in scope. Recognizing this wide range of interests and purpose, this book has attempted to touch on the very narrow perspective of the home breeder whose interest in the monarch is purely for personal enjoyment and pleasure.

The early chapters of this book were aimed at bringing the novice home breeder safely through their first hands-on experience observing the monarch's full cycle of metamorphosis — egg to caterpillar to chrysalis to butterfly. Subsequent chapters provided much more detail, insights, and hopefully helpful information aimed at making your future breeding experiences even more pleasurable. Fittingly, then, this final chapter will close with picking up where the earlier chapters left off by providing some additional ideas and suggestions that broaden the skillset necessary for successful monarch breeding.

### The Hunt Begins

The female monarch deposits eggs one at a time, usually on the underside of milkweed leaves although they will appear on the leaf tops and flowers from time to time as well.

Whether found on the underside of a wild-growing milkweed plant in an open Midwestern field or in your own backyard butterfly garden, each egg is the beginning of a new generation. The eggs are tiny — not much bigger than the head of a pin — so you will have to look closely. If other monarchs are visible flying around the search area, watch for females going from plant to plant depositing eggs and check the underside of the leaves after they are finished. Do not overlook the tops of the leaves as well as the flowers and new growth, although the majority of the time eggs will be on the underside of the milkweed leaves. Leaves with holes in them are a good indication that there either recently were, or very possibly are, caterpillars already on that plant. There may or may not be more eggs, and, of course, you can also clip any leaves with caterpillars already on them to bring back for observation as well. Once satisfied with your haul, head back to the nursery to set everything up.

## Caterpillar Nursery

The first task is to move the eggs to a new butterfly-safe environment that will provide appropriate nourishment (milkweed) as well as protection from the elements, predators, and even other larger caterpillars. While it is ideal for the eggs to hatch directly on the plant the female butterfly chose for them, it is sometimes impossible to bring an entire plant back to an inside nursery after an off-site egg hunt. In such instances, leaves onto which the eggs are attached can be removed from the plant and taken back to the nursery.

Chewed-up leaves and leaves with holes indicate caterpillars and/or eggs may be present.

Some people like to hatch the eggs first in a smaller container and then move them to a larger cage, terrarium, or enclosure. This can be done very easily by placing a dampened layer of paper towel in the bottom of a plastic container. Place the leaves, egg side up, on the paper towel and cover so that the moisture can be retained. It will take approximately three to five days for the eggs to hatch, so they should be monitored daily. If the paper towel seems to be drying out, spray with a light mist from a water bottle. If the leaves become very brittle and dry before the eggs have hatched, carefully clip around the egg(s) with a scissors, taking care not to damage the egg. Allowing a narrow 1/8-inch edge all around is adequate. Re-line the container with a fresh, damp paper towel lined with fresh leaves. Use a tweezers to carefully place each piece of leaf with its egg attached on top of the new leaves and reseal. Continue to check regularly until the hatchlings begin to appear. Remember that they will be within a day of hatching when they turn black on top.

Clip off unhatched eggs and move to fresh, new leaves daily until hatched.

Other people prefer to place the egg — leaf and all — next to a stalk of a milkweed plant to strategically position the emerging caterpillar near its food source. Either option works well, but be sure to disinfect the eggs as well as avoid putting any tiny eggs in a cage where larger caterpillars might be present and already eating every leaf in sight, including any with tiny eggs attached!

Eggs can hatch on the plant selected by the mother.

In terms of butterfly cages, some people find that glass and plastic terrariums work well, while others prefer net enclosures. Both will do the trick, although we have found the Butterfly Screenroom to be the most versatile nursery arrangement for a number of reasons. It has been designed to fit an entire potted plant or plants that will feed and nurture caterpillars from the egg until they are ready to pupate, and the wooden frame is the ideal surface for this purpose. Screened sides and top allow for viewing from all angles, while the hinged door enables an easy swap-out of chewed-up plants for fresher ones. It is easy enough to clean in a large tub and can be either hosed off or immersed to rinse.

**BUTTERFLY SCREENROOM:** Provides full visibility and makes it easy to swap out host plants

Daily monitoring of the eggs will reveal a slight change on the last day as the top of each egg will turn black just before the baby caterpillar emerges. Once completely emerged, the tiny pale-green caterpillar with its completely black head will eat the protein-rich shell before moving onto its first taste of milkweed. At this point, the tiny caterpillar will be about the size of a grain of rice and have very faint black, yellow, and white stripes just barely becoming visible. It will also need to find milkweed readily available, otherwise it may begin exploring and move away from its food source and die because it cannot find its way back to the only nourishment it can eat.

Growth will be quick from this point forward, and in 10 to 14 days, your caterpillar will begin its journey to find an ideal place to pupate. Once attached in its "J" position, it will hang another 10 to 14 hours before it begins its transition to a chrysalis — an amazing thing to witness at least once but usually tricky to catch at the exact moment it happens.

Over the course of the next 10 to 14 days, the most amazing transformation will occur as the chubby little caterpillar bursts out into the world as a beautiful North American monarch ready to make its own contribution to the remarkable legacy of this "King of all Butterflies"!

Thank you for doing your part to help this beautiful but struggling species keep flying across the blue skies of North America. Please spread the word and make others aware of how important it is for everyone to do whatever they can to help keep the North American monarch off of the endangered species list in 2020.

# GLOSSARY

**abdomen** The elongated back part of the body, located behind the thorax.

**aposematic defense** Built-in toxic or dangerous attribute that is used to protect from potential prey.

**bursa** Sac located on female butterfly that stores sperm deposited there by the male until it is needed.

**cardenolides** Toxic steroids in milkweed plants that is passed on to monarch caterpillars.

**caterpillar** Second stage of metamorphosis that follows the egg stage. Also called *larva*.

**chemoreceptor** Cells that can sense chemicals and then relay the message to the rest of the body. In addition to detecting taste and smell, females also have extra chemoreceptors on their legs that detect milkweed.

**chitlin** Protein material in butterfly wings similar to that found in human hair and nails.

**chrysalis** The third stage of metamorphosis that follows the larval stage (caterpillar) and transforms into the adult butterfly. Also called *pupa*.

**citizen scientist** Person who voluntarily contributes time and resources to scientific research either alone or together with professionals.

**clasper** Grasping organ used by the male butterfly to connect to the female during reproduction.

**cremaster** Black stem located on the top of a chrysalis.

*Danaus plexippus* Scientific name for monarch butterfly.

**deforestation** Reduction in forested areas, especially in Mexico.

**diapause** Temporary stage of development in monarchs where they postpone sexual activities to prepare for their migration and overwintering.

**eastern population** Monarch population living to the east of the Rocky Mountains.

**eclose** To emerge from a chrysalis.

**egg** First stage of metamorphosis.

**endangered species** A species in danger of extinction.

**exoskeleton** Hard skeleton-like protective layer on an invertebrate's outer body.

**flyway** Route followed by migrating monarchs either to overwintering site or returning from it.

**frass** Waste product produced by caterpillars (larvae).

**habitat** Natural home of an animal or plant.

**host plant** A plant that provides the necessary food that butterfly offspring (caterpillars) need to survive.

**instar** A period of development.

**J shape** The 12- to 14-hour period just before chrysalis formation when the larval monarch hangs in a shape that resembles the letter "J."

**Johnston's organ** Unique to butterflies, an organ that controls balance and is responsible for a butterfly's ability to right itself on a windy day.

**larva** Second stage of metamorphosis that follows the egg stage. Also called *caterpillar*.

**Lepidoptera** Order of insects to which butterflies and moths belong.

**life cycle** Stages of development, which are the egg, caterpillar, chrysalis, and butterfly.

*Lespesia archippivora (La)* Parasitic tachinid fly prevalent in monarchs.

**Linnaeus, Carl** Swedish botanist, physician, and zoologist (b. 1707, d. 1778) who developed the system for naming and organizing organisms.

**Malpighian tubules** Part of a butterfly's excretory system.

**maxillary palps** Sensory organs that direct food into a caterpillar's mouth.

**metamorphosis** Developmental process for insects that includes egg to caterpillar to chrysalis to adult butterfly.

**migration** Seasonal movement of animals; annual movement of monarchs from all over North America southward in the winter and northward when the warmer weather returns.

**milkweed** Plants in the *Asclepias* family that are the sole food source for insects in the *Danaus* genus classification.

**molting** Shedding of outer skin to facilitate rapid growth from instar to instar.

**native plants** Plants that occur naturally in an area and have done so for many years.

**nectar plant** Flowering plants that provide food in the form of nectar for adult butterflies and other pollinators.

**non-migratory** Species that do not participate in seasonal migration.

**nuclear polyhedrosis virus (NPV)** Deadly virus that affects months and butterflies. Also called "Black Death," "Wilt," and "Melt."

**ocelli** Caterpillar's simple eyes.

*Ophryocystis elektroscirrha (OE)* Spore-producing protozoan parasite that infects butterflies in the *Danaus* species group; i.e., those that eat milkweed, including the monarch, queen, and soldier butterflies.

**oyamel forest** A Mexican forest of oyamel fir trees where monarchs overwinter.

**overwintering** Migrating to another location for survival.

*P. cassotis* A tiny wasp that parasitizes monarchs.

**parasite** Organisms that live on or inside the body of another organism, depending on it for all of the nutrition and resources necessary for their own life cycle.

**pathogen** Organism that causes disease, including bacteria, viruses, and parasites.

**pollinator** An animal that moves pollen from one plant to another and in so doing causes it to make fruit or seeds.

**predator** An animal that survives by killing, hurting, or eating other animals.

**proboscis** Straw-like feeding tube used by adult butterflies to suck nectar from flowers.

**proleg** False legs located on the caterpillar's abdominal segments.

**puddling** When butterflies seek out moist, muddy, fermenting fruit and other plant matter to suck up sodium (salt) and other needed minerals.

**pupa** Same as *chrysalis*.

**pupate** The process of a larva (caterpillar) changing to a pupa (chrysalis).

**roost** Perch, sit, or rest, such as when migrating monarchs stop during their journey.

**scales** Dusty-looking modified hairs located on monarch wings that are involved in both bright coloring and attraction of the opposite sex.

**scent gland** Dark dots on a male monarch's hind wings from which a chemical is secreted to attract female monarchs.

**spiracles** Breathing spores located on the monarch's abdomen.

**tachinid fly** Tiny parasitic fly that lays its eggs on the outer skin of a monarch caterpillar. When the eggs hatch, the tiny larval hatchlings bore into the host caterpillar, where they fully develop and emerge later during late larva or early pupa stage as maggots.

**thermals** Upper air masses used by monarchs during migratory flights.

**thorax** One of three body parts of a butterfly's body to which legs and wings are attached.

**western population** Monarch population living to the west of the Rocky Mountains.

# INDEX

Image: Fall & Spring Migration Map
US Fish and Wildlife Service

# RESOURCES

**Butterfly Screenrooms**
bfliesboca@gmail.com
Wooden cages with hinged doors
Email inquires welcome

**CitizenScience.org**
https://www.citizenscience.org/
Variety of ways to involve the public in
scientific research

**Journey North**
https://journeynorth.org/monarchs
Migration news and tracking maps;
teaching tools for educators

**Monarch Joint Venture**
www.monarchjointventure.org
Partnership of state and federal
agencies, not-for-profit organizations,
businesses, and academia pooling
efforts to protect monarch and pollinator
habitats across the United States

**Monarch Watch**
https://www.monarchwatch.org
Key information and links; information
and resources for educators; tagging
programs; creating certified Waystations

**Monarch Watch Waystations**
https://www.monarchwatch.org/
waystations/download.html
Program aimed at creating, conserving,
and protecting monarch habitats

**National Wildlife Foundation**
www.nwf.org
Non-profit conservation and education
advocacy organization

**Native Plant Vendors, Directory of**
www.plantmilkweed.org
Link to Monarch Joint Venture's
milkweed information page; includes
links for native seed and plant sources

**Save Our Monarchs**
https://www.saveourmonarchs.org
Non-profit organization dedicated
to saving the monarch by promoting
habitat conservation and milkweed-
planting programs

**Stewardship Garden**
https://www.ourhabitatgarden.org/
creatures/milkweed-growing.html
Guide to collecting and planting
milkweed seeds and much more

**University of Minnesota Monarch
Lab**
https://monarchlab.org
Wealth of information about monarch
research, education, and gardening

**USDA**
https://planthardiness.ars.usda.gov/
PHZMWeb/
Provides a Plant Hardiness Zone Map to
help determine which plants are best for
any given area

**US Fish & Wildlife Service**
http://www.fws.gov/savethemonarch
Governmental agency doing analysis
to determine if the monarch should be
classified an Endangered Species; good
source for information and links

**Xerces Society**
https://xerces.org/monarchs/
International non-profit promotes
conservation of invertebrate and their
habitats, including the monarch

https://xerces.org/milkweed-seed-finder/
Comprehensive national directory of
milkweed vendors and seed sources

## ACKNOWLEDGMENTS

**M**any thanks to my family and friends for their patience, indulgence, and encouragement while I placed everyone and everything on hold to finally put into writing the book I have carried around in my head for so long!

I am especially grateful to my good friend of many years, Celida Ford, who first introduced me to her "hobby" nearly twenty years ago. Without that introduction, I would never have realized the joy and satisfaction that comes with learning to appreciate butterflies of all types, but especially the monarch. My yard would also probably be pretty bland if knowledge of so many different and beautiful flowering plants wasn't also a secondary benefit of learning to raise and conserve butterflies!

It is my sincere hope that you, too, will find the pleasure that I have found through butterfly gardening and conservation. Along with that, however, is my greatest desire that others will come away with additional inspiration to actively participate in habitat restoration and conservation and in so doing help keep the monarch off of the Endangered Species list.

*Holly Urie*

USDA/NRCS

### Photo Credits
Unless otherwise indicated underneath the photo or image, all photos and images were taken from the author's personal stock.

## ABOUT THE AUTHOR

**H**olly Urie is a native Midwesterner, born and raised in the Chicago suburb of Hillside. She graduated from Western Illinois University in 1974 and moved to South Florida in 1975, where she and her husband raised their three children and reside today.

Holly has always had a love for nature, the out of doors, and above all, animals and critters of every kind. As mentioned in the acknowledgments, she was introduced to the monarch by her friend, Celida, a number of years ago, and "the rest is history" as the saying goes. An avid softball coach and former softball player in her spare time, her hands-on experience with butterflies expanded when she started designing and building butterfly cages for the younger siblings of softball players on her teams. They were a hit; and there was so much immediate demand for them, she eventually began to offer them online as well. As the designs have become more sophisticated over the years, so too has the depth of her own knowledge of butterflies — monarchs in particular — as each cage included milkweed plants loaded with caterpillars (except for those sold online) along with a small instruction sheet she gradually developed.

That instruction sheet has now morphed into this book. While certainly not a complete scientific presentation of the species, hopefully there is enough information to pique the interest of readers and be a source of inspiration for others wishing to contribute to the critical movement to Save the Monarch.

Made in the USA
Columbia, SC
29 June 2021